SCIENCE EXPLORER

COMPOUNDS

AND MIXTURES

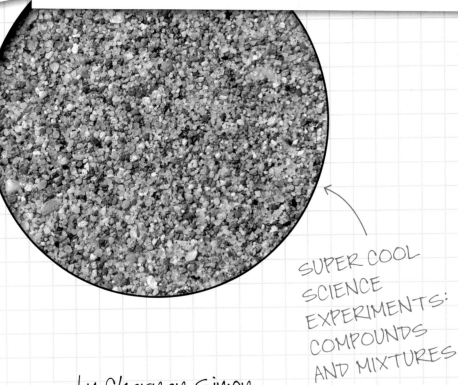

SUPER COOL
SCIENCE
EXPERIMENTS:
COMPOUNDS
AND MIXTURES

by Charnan Simon

CHERRY LAKE PUBLISHING • ANN ARBOR, MICHIGAN

CHERRY
LAKE
Publishing

A NOTE TO PARENTS AND TEACHERS: Please review the instructions for these experiments before your children do them. Be sure to help them with any experiments you do not think they can safely conduct on their own.

A NOTE TO KIDS: Be sure to ask an adult for help with these experiments when you need it. Always put your safety first!

Published in the United States of America by
Cherry Lake Publishing
Ann Arbor, Michigan
www.cherrylakepublishing.com

Content Editor: Robert Wolffe, EdD,
Professor of Teacher Education,
Bradley University, Peoria, Illinois

Book design and illustration: The Design Lab

Grateful acknowledgment to Deborah Simon, Department of Chemistry,
Whitman College

Photo Credits: Cover and page 1, ©Fenton, used under license
from Shutterstock, Inc.; page 5, ©iStockphoto.com/AVAVA; page 7,
©iStockphoto.com/Jbryson; page 8, ©vladoleg, used under license from
Shutterstock, Inc.; page 12, ©Celso Pupo, used under license from
Shutterstock, Inc.; page 16, ©iStockphoto.com/RBFried; page 20, © April
Turner, used under license from Shutterstock, Inc.; page 24, ©Scott
Rothstein, used under license from Shutterstock, Inc.

Library of Congress Cataloging-in-Publication Data
Simon, Charnan.
  Super cool science experiments: Compounds and mixtures /
by Charnan Simon.
    p. cm.—(Science explorer)
  Includes bibliographical references and index.
  ISBN-13: 978-1-60279-536-5   ISBN-10: 1-60279-536-3 (lib. bdg.)
  ISBN-13: 978-1-60279-615-7   ISBN-10: 1-60279-615-7 (pbk.)
  1. Chemical reactions—Experiments—Juvenile literature. 2. Organic
compounds—Juvenile literature. I. Title. II. Title: Compounds and
mixtures. III. Series.
  QD501.S5827 2010
  540.78—dc22

                                    2009008680

Cherry Lake Publishing would like to acknowledge the work
of The Partnership for 21st Century Skills. Please visit
www.21stcenturyskills.org for more information.

SCIENCE EXPLORER

COMPOUNDS AND MIXTURES

TABLE OF CONTENTS

Mixtures Are Everywhere!

Think of a jar of gumballs. You see many colors. The gumballs can be mixed in the jar in many different combinations. Even so, they are not joined together in a special way. Would you believe that this jar of gumballs represents something scientific? In a way, the gumballs form a simple mixture.

Have you ever wondered about the many mixtures that are around you? If so, you are on your way to thinking like a scientist. Did you know that you can run experiments using materials you have at home? In this book, we'll learn how scientists think. We'll do that by experimenting with mixtures and compounds. We'll find out just what mixtures and compounds are and how they are different. We'll even learn how to make our own experiments!

First Things First

↖ Let's cook up some compounds and mixtures!

Scientists learn by studying something very carefully. For example, scientists who study mixtures and compounds know that some substances mix easily and some don't. Some substances dissolve in a solution. Sometimes when two substances mix, there's a chemical reaction. A whole new substance is created. Scientists do experiments to see how these reactions happen.

Good scientists take notes on everything they discover. They write down their observations. Sometimes those observations lead scientists to ask new questions. With new questions in mind, they design experiments to find the answers.

When scientists design experiments, they must think very clearly. The way they think about problems is often called the scientific method. What is the scientific method? It's a step-by-step way of finding answers to specific questions. The steps don't always follow the same pattern. Sometimes scientists change their minds. The process often works something like this:

Scientific method

- **Step One:** A scientist gathers the facts and makes observations about one particular thing.
- **Step Two:** The scientist comes up with a question that is not answered by all the observations and facts.
- **Step Three:** The scientist creates a hypothesis. This is a statement of what the scientist thinks is probably the answer to the question.
- **Step Four:** The scientist tests the hypothesis. He or she designs an experiment to see whether the hypothesis is correct. The scientist does the experiment and writes down what happens.
- **Step Five:** The scientist draws a conclusion based on how the experiment turned out. The

conclusion might be that the hypothesis is correct. Sometimes, though, the hypothesis is not correct. In that case, the scientist might develop a new hypothesis and another experiment.

In the following experiments, we'll see the scientific method in action. We'll gather some facts and observations about compounds and mixtures. And for each experiment, we'll develop a question and a hypothesis. Next, we'll do an actual experiment to see if our hypothesis is correct. By the end of the experiment, we should know something new about compounds and mixtures. Scientists, are you ready? Then let's get started!

↰ The scientific method can help you
answer all kinds of questions.

Experiment #1
Mix It Up

First, let's gather some observations. What do you already know about mixtures? You probably know the basics: a mixture is a blend of two or more substances.

This observation leads us to several questions. What happens when you try to mix one substance with another? Do the two substances stay separate? Can they be unmixed? Come up with a hypothesis about separating the parts of a mixture. Here is

A mixture can be as simple as a handful of nuts.

one option: **Some substances stay separate when mixed and can be unmixed.** Now you can set up an experiment to test the hypothesis.

Here's what you'll need:
- 1 tablespoon of dried beans
- 3 tablespoons of sand
- 4 small bowls
- 1 tablespoon of small pebbles
- 1 tablespoon of salt
- 1 tablespoon each of green and red sugar sprinkles
- Kitchen colander
- Baking sheet

Do you have everything you need?

Instructions:
1. Pour the dried beans and 1 tablespoon of sand in a bowl. Pour the pebbles and 1 tablespoon of sand in another bowl. Add 1 tablespoon of sand and the salt to the third bowl. Pour the green and red sugar sprinkles in the fourth bowl.

Be sure to write down what you observe.

2. Stir the substances to mix them together. How does each mixture look?

3. Place the colander on the baking sheet. Carefully pour the sand and beans mixture into the colander. Gently tap the colander with your hand. What happens? Does some of the sand fall through the holes onto the cookie sheet? Do the larger beans stay behind in the colander?

4. Empty the colander.

5. Pour the sand and pebbles mixture through the colander. What passes through and what doesn't?

6. Empty the colander, and test the sand and salt mixture the same way. Do both materials pass through?

7. Test the mixture of sugar sprinkles the same way, and observe what passes through the colander.

Conclusion:
What did you notice about the four mixtures you created in the bowls? Did the substances keep

their individual characteristics even after being mixed? Could you still see beans and sand, pebbles and sand, salt and sand, and red and green sugar sprinkles?

We used the colander as a tool to help us unmix the materials. Did the colander separate the substances in all four mixtures? The holes in the colander may have been too large to separate the finer ingredients. Both the red and green sugar might have been able to fall through the holes onto the baking sheet. How about the sand and salt? Depending on the type of colander, the holes might have been too small to let all of the sand or other fine particles through. But that doesn't mean the materials can't be separated. Can you think of different ways to separate materials that the colander couldn't? Was your hypothesis correct?

Sometimes it is easy to separate a mixture. Sometimes it is difficult. It would be hard work, but you could separate the sand from the salt, or the red sugar sprinkles from the green ones. One way to do this is by hand. The bits of sand, salt, and colored sprinkles are still present in the mixtures. They haven't been changed into something different. The substances making up a mixture are not chemically combined. They can be separated using physical means.

Experiment #2 What's the Solution?

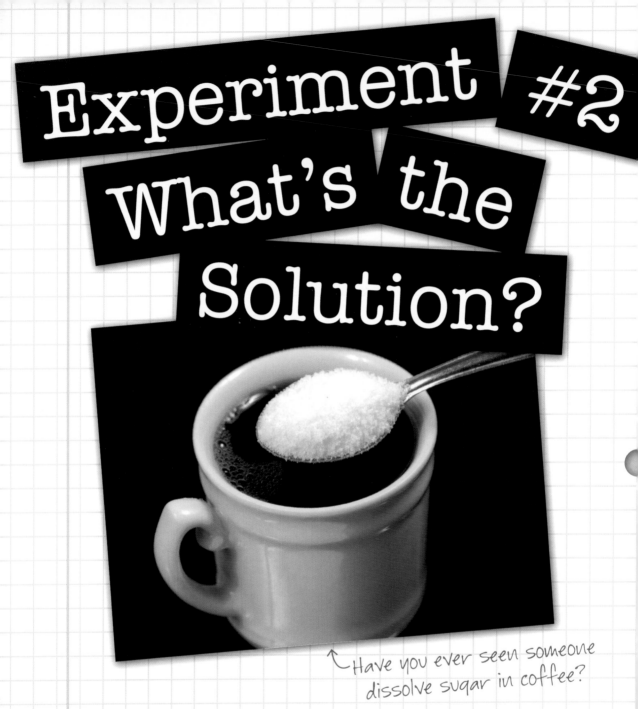

↖ Have you ever seen someone dissolve sugar in coffee?

You've seen what happens when you mix solid substances together. A solution is another common type of mixture. It is made up of a solute (something that dissolves, usually a solid) mixed with a solvent (a substance, usually a liquid, that will dissolve other substances). Is it possible to add a solute such as sugar to a solvent such as water? Would this form a mixture that is homogeneous, or the same throughout?

Let's try it and find out! Our hypothesis will be: **The addition of sugar to water will form a homogeneous solution**.

Here's what you'll need:

- Spoon
- Drinking glass
- Dishwashing liquid
- Water
- Paper towel
- Distilled water
- 1 teaspoon of sugar
- Drinking straw

You probably have most of these materials in your kitchen.

Instructions:

1. Wash the spoon and glass in soapy water. Rinse them, and then dry them with a paper towel.
2. Fill the glass halfway with distilled water.
3. Add the sugar, and stir until no particles can be seen.
4. Set the drinking straw in the sugar water. Hold your finger over the top of the straw as you raise it out of the glass (this will keep the mixture in the straw). Taste the liquid. Remember how sweet it tastes.
5. Use the straw to taste samples from the bottom, middle, and top of the glass. Compare the taste of the mixture samples.

Which sample is the sweetest? Record your results.

Conclusion:

Do the samples all have the same level of sweetness? Does this mean the solution is evenly mixed?

The solute (sugar) in your solution has dissolved in the solvent (water). The sugar has broken apart into smaller and smaller particles. These particles spread out evenly in the water. The mixture is homogeneous because the sugar molecules and the water molecules are evenly mixed. The samples in your straw contained the same proportion of sugar molecules to water molecules no matter where in the solution they came from. This solution is still a mixture. The sugar molecules and the water molecules have not combined chemically to form a new substance. Was your hypothesis correct?

What would happen if you added more sugar solute to your solution? A solution that will not dissolve any more solute is saturated.

Did you know that solutes don't have to be solids? You've probably had one solution made of a gas dissolved in a liquid: soda. Solutions can also be gases dissolved in other gases and liquids dissolved in other liquids. If you mix things and they stay in even distribution, it's a solution.

Experiment #3

Suspend It!

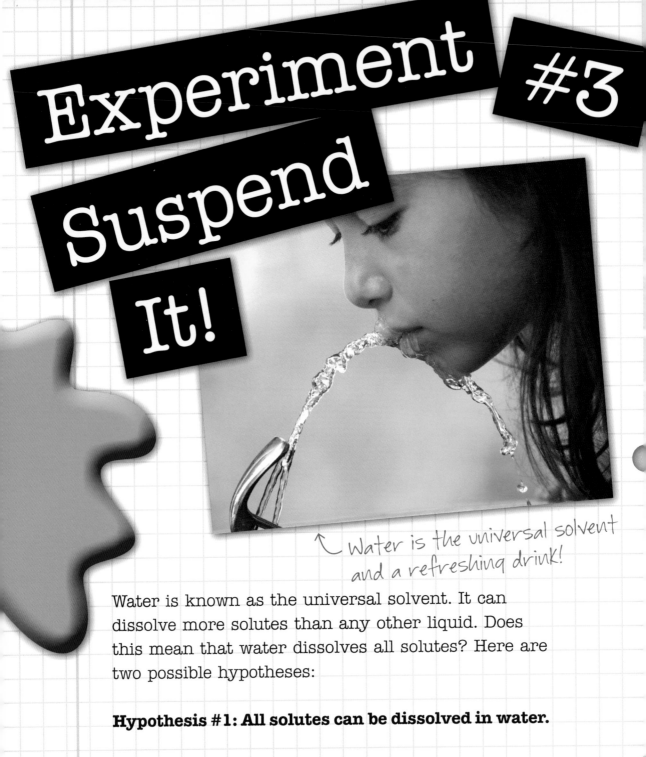

← Water is the universal solvent and a refreshing drink!

Water is known as the universal solvent. It can dissolve more solutes than any other liquid. Does this mean that water dissolves all solutes? Here are two possible hypotheses:

Hypothesis #1: All solutes can be dissolved in water.

Hypothesis #2: Some, but not all, solutes can be dissolved in water.

Here's what you'll need:

- Tablespoon
- Soil
- 3 clear jars, with lids, that are the same size
- Flour
- Salt
- Water

You don't have to buy soil if you can get some from your backyard.

Instructions:

1. Put 2 tablespoons of soil in a jar. Put 2 tablespoons of flour in the second jar. Add 2 tablespoons of salt to the third jar.

2. Fill each jar with water, and screw the lids on tightly. Shake each jar energetically 10 times.
3. Put the jars on a tabletop. Let them sit undisturbed for 30 minutes. Observe the contents of the jars every 5 minutes.

Shake it up!

Conclusion:
What happens in each jar? The salt dissolves in water. But as soon as you stop shaking the other two jars, gravity starts pulling the soil and the flour down. The heavier soil particles settle first. The smaller flour

particles take longer. Both substances are eventually pulled to the bottom of the jars. To really see this in action, observe your soil and flour jars again after 2 hours. Has the water become very clear?

Did you prove your hypothesis? If you chose Hypothesis #2, you did. Water may be called the universal solvent, but it doesn't dissolve everything. Instead of 3 solutions, you've made 1 solution and 2 suspensions. The soil and flour particles spread out, or became suspended, in the water for a while. They eventually settled to the bottom of the jar.

Don't worry if you chose Hypothesis #1, which turned out to be wrong. There isn't a scientist worth his or her salt who hasn't had a hypothesis turn out wrong. Sometimes scientists repeat their experiments over and over to make sure they get the same results. It is not a good idea to trust the results of only one trial of an experiment. Scientists want to be sure that the hypothesis really is correct or incorrect.

Experiment #4
Bring Back the Substances!

Do you think the food coloring can be separated from the water?

A mixture is a blend of 2 or more pure substances (elements or compounds) that are not chemically combined. The mixture can usually be separated into the original components by physical means. You saw one way to separate 2 solid components of a mixture in Experiment #1. Can you also separate substances combined in a solution or a suspension? What do you think?

Here is one hypothesis you might want to test: **Because solutions and suspensions are mixtures, the materials combined in them can be separated.**

Here's what you'll need:

- 2 tablespoons of flour
- 2 tablespoons of salt
- Clear drinking glass, washed and dried
- Clean spoon
- Hot tap water
- Coffee filter

- Wide-mouthed jar
- Rubber band
- Shallow dish

Looking for a jar? Check your family's recycling bin.

Instructions:

1. Add the flour and salt to the glass. Stir well to mix them.
2. Fill the glass with hot tap water. Stir well. Let the glass sit for 20 minutes.
3. Collect a spoonful of the water, and taste a bit of it. How does it taste? What happened to the flour? Record your observations.

Pour slowly!

4. Put the coffee filter over the top of the wide-mouthed jar. Let the filter sag a little into the middle of the jar. Hold the sides of the filter in place by stretching the rubber band over the mouth of the jar.

5. Stir your water mixture to put the flour back in suspension. Pour some of the liquid onto the filter. Pour slowly to allow the water to drip through the filter. You might need to add a little hot tap water to help things along. What happens? Record your observations.

6. Pour some of the liquid that passes through the filter into the shallow dish. Set the dish on a sunny windowsill until all of the water disappears. This may take several days. What do you see in the dish once all of the water is gone?

Conclusion:

Were you able to separate the parts of a solution and suspension? Was your hypothesis correct?

During step #2, the salt dissolved in the water to form a solution. That's why the water at the top of the glass tastes salty. The flour stayed suspended in the water for a while. It eventually settled to the bottom of the glass. That's what the white stuff is. The particles in a suspension are too large to fit in the spaces between the molecules of water. The bits do not dissolve, and the mixture may appear murky or cloudy. They settle when the mixture sits. You've created a solution and a suspension in one glass!

Are coffee filters an effective way to separate the mixture? The flour particles are too large to pass through the filter, and they collect as white stuff on top. The salt particles are small enough to pass through the filter. The saltwater solution collects in the jar. Using filters is one physical way of separating the parts of a mixture.

The water in the solution you placed near the sunny window should have eventually evaporated. Evaporation is the process in which a liquid changes to a gas or vapor. The salt crystals are left behind in the dish. Evaporation is another physical way of separating a mixture.

Your hypothesis is correct! You've separated out the original substances that made up your solution and suspension. The flour remains in the filter, the salt is in the shallow dish, and the water has evaporated into the air. Good job, junior scientist!

Experiment #5

Compound the Fun

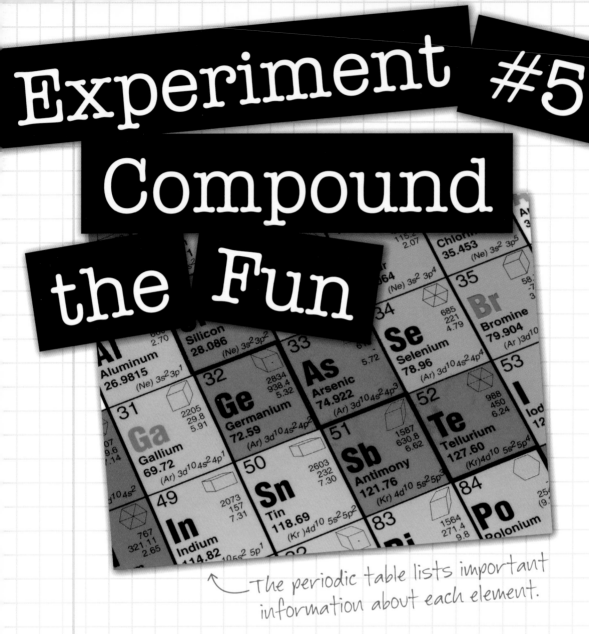

↙ The periodic table lists important information about each element.

So far, we've done experiments with various types of mixtures. Now it's time to investigate compounds. A compound is a combination of two or more elements. Elements are substances that cannot be separated into simpler substances using chemistry. When the elements combine, there is a chemical reaction on the molecular level. The resulting compound is a completely new substance. It cannot be changed back to its original elements by simple physical means.

Think about something you see every day: water. It is a compound. Hydrogen and oxygen are colorless gases. These elements can act together to form water.

There are many different kinds of chemical reactions. This experiment will combine two elements to make a homemade volcanic eruption. What do you think will happen when vinegar and baking soda come together? Our hypothesis is: **A chemical reaction will take place when baking soda is combined with vinegar, resulting in a new substance.**

Here's what you'll need:
- Safety goggles
- Red food coloring
- 1 cup of white vinegar
- Funnel
- 1 tablespoon of baking soda
- Small plastic bottle
- Large tray
- Dirt, sand, and gravel

Safety glasses help protect your eyes.

Instructions:

1. Put on your safety goggles. Add 5 drops of red food coloring to the cup of vinegar.
2. Use the funnel to pour the baking soda into the plastic bottle. Place the bottle in the middle of the tray.
3. Pile dirt, sand, and gravel around the bottle. You are forming the cone of your volcano. Leave the hole of the bottle uncovered, and be careful not to spill dirt in it!
4. Use the funnel to quickly pour all of the colored vinegar into the bottle. What happens next?

Look out! Exploding volcano!

Conclusion:

Did your volcano erupt? Did a bubbly or frothy mixture ooze out? What could have caused the change in your materials? Did you prove your hypothesis?

You might have been able to hear a faint gassy, hissing sound as the baking soda and vinegar came into contact with each other. The baking soda reacts chemically with the vinegar. In the process, a new substance is produced: carbon dioxide gas. This gas builds up enough pressure inside the bottle to force the red liquid out the top. The mixture of gas and liquid produces the foam.

One way to help you better understand the changes involved with compounds is to think of a cake. The eggs, flour, sugar, and other ingredients are all mixed and combined. Pretend these ingredients are elements. When a cake comes out of the oven, does it look or seem much like the component elements that it is made of? Have changes taken place that would make it difficult to turn that cake back into the original eggs, flour, sugar, and other ingredients?

Experiment #6
Do It Yourself!

You might have heard someone say, "Those two are like oil and water!" The person was probably talking about two people who just don't get along. Is there some science behind that expression? Do oil and water not "get along"?

Scientists know that some liquids are immiscible. That means they do not mix. They separate into layers. Some liquids are miscible. They can be mixed. Do you think cooking oil and water are immiscible liquids? Come up with a hypothesis. What would you need to run an experiment and test the hypothesis?

Okay, scientists! Now you know many things about mixtures and compounds. You learned through your observations and experiments. You saw how one experiment can raise and answer lots of different questions. You even learned how to make your very own volcano! Isn't being a scientist fun?

How would you experiment with oil and water?

An emulsion is a mixture of immiscible liquids. Scientists also know that some things can be added to emulsions to help them stay stable and mixed. These things are called emulsifying agents. These agents help prevent the emulsion from separating into layers.

Soap is one emulsifying agent. Did you find that oil and water are immiscible liquids? If so, would adding drops of dishwashing detergent to the mixture affect how the liquids behave? There's only one way to find out. Gather your supplies, come up with a hypothesis, and write down the steps of your experiment. Then comes the fun part. Run your own experiment, and discover what happens!

Adding emulsifying agents to some mixtures, and then mixing well, can create a kind of mixture called a colloid. You actually know of lots of colloids, although you may not know that you know them! Homogenized milk is a colloid. Mayonnaise is a colloid. Marshmallows and shaving cream are colloids, too. The individual particles are still there in a colloidal mixture, but they're harder to separate out. You can only see them with a powerful microscope.

GLOSSARY

colloid (KOL-oid) a substance made of tiny particles that do not dissolve but remain suspended in a gas, liquid, or solid

compounds (KOM-poundz) substances in which elements are bound to each other in a definite ratio of each element

conclusion (kuhn-KLOO-zhuhn) a final decision, thought, or opinion

homogeneous (hoh-muh-JEEN-ee-yuhss) uniformly the same throughout

hypothesis (hy-POTH-uh-sihss) a logical guess about what will happen in an experiment

immiscible (i-MISS-uh-buhl) incapable of being mixed

method (METH-uhd) a way of doing something

miscible (MISS-uh-buhl) capable of being mixed

observations (ob-zur-VAY-shuhnz) things that are seen or noticed with one's senses

solution (suh-LOO-shuhn) a mixture in which the molecule-sized particles of a solute are evenly spread out among the solvent molecules

suspensions (suh-SPEN-shuhnz) mixtures in which tiny particles remain suspended in a liquid or gas without dissolving

FOR MORE INFORMATION

BOOKS

Aloian, Molly. *Mixtures and Solutions.* New York: Crabtree Publishing, 2009.

Hauser, Jill Frankel. *Super Science Concoctions: 50 Mysterious Mixtures for Fabulous Fun.* Nashville: Williamson Books, 2007.

Kjelle, Marylou Morano. *Mixtures and Compounds.* New York: PowerKids Press, 2007.

WEB SITES

BBC—Science: Chemistry: Compounds

www.bbc.co.uk/schools/ks3bitesize/science/chemistry/elements_com_mix_3.shtml
Learn more about compounds

BBC—Science: Chemistry: Separating Mixtures

www.bbc.co.uk/schools/ks3bitesize/science/chemistry/elements_com_mix_8.shtml
Watch short animations that show how scientists separate the parts of different mixtures

PBS Kids—ZOOMsci: Cauldron Bubbles

pbskids.org/zoom/activities/sci/cauldronbubbles.html
Run another experiment involving oil and water

INDEX

About the → Author

Charnan Simon is a former editor of *Cricket* magazine and the author of more than 100 books for young readers. She lives in Seattle, Washington, and is learning more about chemistry every day.